LETTERS FROM MEDIEVAL CHRISTIAN NORTH AFRICA

LETTERS FROM MEDIEVAL CHRISTIAN NORTH AFRICA

Copyright 2024 by Dalcassian Press

All rights reserved. No part of this book may be reproduced in any manner whatsoever without written permission except in the case of brief quotations embodied in critical articles and reviews.

No part of this publication may be reproduced, distributed, or transmitted in any form or by any means, including photocopying, recording, or other electronic or mechanical methods, without the prior written permission of the publisher, except in the case of brief quotations embodied in critical reviews and certain other non-commercial uses permitted by copyright law. For permission request, write to Dalcassian Press at admin@thescriptoriumproject.com

Translator: Curtin, D.P. (1985-)

ISBN: 979-8-3302-0329-1 (Paperback)
ISBN: 979-8-3302-0925-5 (eBook)
Library of Congress Control Number:

Printed by Ingram Content Group, 1 Ingram Blvd, La Vergne, Tennessee
First Printing 2024, Dalcassian Press, Wilmington, DE

This work is part of a series produced in association with the Scriptorium Project and its community of scholars and translators.
Please visit our website at: www.thescriptoriumproject.com

INTRODUCTION

The history of the Latin Church in North Africa following the Arab conquest of the 7th century represents one of the most significant episodes of ecclesiastical decline in the history of Christendom. Rarely is the idea of a defunct church found in the history of Christian civilization, but the Punic church resides as an uncommon episode in the cultural, intellectual, and religious decline of a once thriving branch of Christendom Once a vibrant center of Christian life, theology, and ecclesial authority, North Africa—home to figures such as Tertullian, St. Cyprian, and St. Augustine—underwent a protracted and complex process of religious transformation as it passed into Muslim political control. From the initial Islamic incursions in the 640s through the consolidation of Arab rule by the early 8th century, the region's Christian communities faced an evolving set of challenges, including shifting demographics, diminishing institutional support, increasing isolation from Western Christendom, and gradual assimilation into the Islamic cultural and religious environment.

The Arab-Muslim conquest of North Africa, which began in earnest during the caliphate of 'Uthmān (r. 644–656) and culminated with the fall of Carthage in 699 AD, marked the beginning of the end for Roman and political authority in the region. Prior to this, the Latin Church in North Africa had already undergone significant challenges, including the theological turmoil of the Donatist schism, the Vandal occupation in the 5th century, and earlier persecutions under the political zeal of the Emperor Diocletian. Nevertheless, despite these tensions, the Lati-Punic episcopate remained broadly intact, with bishops presiding over well-organized dioceses and maintaining strong liturgical and theological traditions that traced their origins to the foundation of Christianity. The Arab conquest did not immediately eradicate these structures, or even make a considerable dent into their public perception. Rather, in the initial decades following the conquest, the new Muslim authorities often permitted the continued existence of Christian communities, consistent with Islamic legal traditions that accorded protected status (dhimma) to "People of the Book."

Indeed, evidence from this transitional period suggests that Christian bishops, monasteries, and lay communities continued to function under Arab rule, especially in more rural and mountainous areas. Notably, the 7th-century Christian apologetic texts from North Africa in Latin and African Romance, reveal that Christians continued to articulate their faith in the face of Islamic dominance and engaged in theological disputation. These texts are among the last literary witnesses to a North African Latin Christianity that had not yet succumbed to extinction. Archeological evidence, including the continued use of church buildings, tomb stones, and inscriptions in Latin, also suggests that the ecclesial infrastructure persisted at least into the 9th century in certain metropolitan localities.

Yet, the broader trajectory was unmistakably one of decline. A key factor was the severing of institutional ties with the wider Western Church. The Arab conquest created a communications and logistical barrier between North African Christians and the See of Rome. Unlike the Eastern Christians in the Levant, who could appeal to the Byzantine Empire or continue to benefit from a strong monastic network, Latin Christians in North Africa were left politically and theologically orphaned. This lack of external support hastened the erosion of episcopal succession, as bishops died or were forcibly converted and were not replaced. Without a robust episcopate, the sacramental and pastoral life of communities began to wither. By the 10th century, there is little evidence of an active Latin ecclesiastical hierarchy in the region. The few letters from after this period note the state of the Punic church as being in tatters, consisting of no more than a handful of remaining bishops.

Moreover, the slow but persistent process of Arabization and Islamization altered the cultural environment in which Christianity had once flourished. Over generations, Latin as a spoken and liturgical language fell into disuse, replaced by Arabic as the *lingua franca* of both state administration and common daily life. The Christian communities that remained adopted Arabic for communication and increasingly absorbed Islamic modes of thought and practice. Conversion to Islam was politically, financially and culturally attractive, and the pressure applied by Arab authorities steadily reduced the Christian population. The dhimmi status, while offering protection, also imposed heavy taxation, segregation, and legal inferiority on Christians, placing a long-term burden on Christians and encouraging assimilation into the Arab world. This decline culminated in the destruction of the cultural edifice of Latin-Punic North Africa, the catalysts of which remain mysterious, as there is little surviving of the Latin or Punic tongues in the Arab or Berber dialects that survive in the region. Instead, the only surviving remnant of African Romance, as St. Augustine would have known it is on the island of Sardinia.

Nonetheless, there is evidence that isolated Christian communities survived into the 12th and even 13th centuries in certain pockets of North Africa, outside of the cosmopolitan influence of Arab princes and merchants. Arab geographers and chroniclers, such as al-Bakrī and Ibn Khaldūn, reference Christian populations and churches, especially in areas such as the Aurès Mountains and near Qayrawān. A famous example is the reference to a Christian bishop in Qayrawān during the time of the Zirid dynasty (10th–11th centuries), suggesting that some episcopal structures may have persisted longer than previously assumed. However, these survivors were exceptionally rare and increasingly marginalized in a hostile state, who saw them as potentially dangerous aliens. By the 11th century, these communities were often Arabic-speaking and bore little resemblance to the flourishing Latin Church of late antiquity. Their rituals and beliefs were sometimes described by contemporaneous Muslim sources as heretical or syncretic, indicating a drift from formal orthodoxy under the pressure of cultural isolation.

Efforts by Latin Christendom to re-establish a presence in North Africa during the Crusading era proved largely ineffective. While the Normans of Sicily briefly occupied coastal cities like Mahdia in the 12th century and attempted to restore Christian worship, these initiatives were temporary and failed to revive local Christian communities in any significant way. The papacy, particularly under Innocent III and later Honorius III, expressed concern about the Christians of North Africa and occasionally sent legates or appealed to rulers to aid them. Yet these efforts lacked sustained support or a coherent strategy and did not reverse the region's ecclesial dissolution. The later Reconquista and Latin missions focused increasingly on Iberia and the Levant, bypassing the Maghreb altogether.

By the 13th century, the Latin Church in North Africa had effectively ceased to exist as a living institution. What remained were only faint traces—place names, ruins of churches, isolated reports of small Christian enclaves, and the writings of earlier centuries. The transformation of North Africa into an overwhelmingly Muslim region, both demographically and culturally, was complete. In ecclesiastical terms, the once-great patriarchate of Carthage had vanished, leaving no successor. Carthage remained a titular see in the Catholic church before being officially dissolved in 1964. Its disappearance marked not only the end of a regional church but also the loss of a distinctive strand of Western Christianity. The legacy of North African Latin Christianity, while preserved in the writings of its great theologians and saints, became a matter of history rather than a feature of contemporary ecclesial life.

The fate of the Latin Church in North Africa from the Arab conquest to the 13th century illustrates a complex process of religious transformation shaped by political, cultural, and theological forces. The initial survival of Christian communities under Islamic rule gave way to a gradual but inexorable decline, culminating in their near-total disappearance by the High Middle Ages. Though punctuated by moments of resilience and faint hope, the Latin Church's extinction in North Africa underscores the profound consequences of religious and civilizational change in the medieval world. It remains a subject of poignant reflection for those Christian communities that lay outside of the jurisdiction of the broader communion, or feel that they can operate independently against the cultural weight of the external world.

SYNOD OF CARTHAGE

Gregory, Archbishop of Carthage
Unknown date, 646 AD

Venerable brothers, defenders of the faith of our Lord Jesus Christ, bishops and priests of the province of Africa, gathered in the Synod of Carthage, greetings in the Lord.

We, the venerable brothers, defenders of the faith of our Lord Jesus Christ, bishops and priests of the province of Africa, gathered in the Synod of Carthage, greet you in the Lord.

Since it has come to our knowledge that certain heretics, the Monothelites, claim that in Christ there is only one will which occupies both the divine and human nature, we have unanimously decreed in this synod, and judged from sacred Scriptures and orthodox tradition of the Church, that there are two wills in one Christ, our Lord Jesus Christ: namely, a divine will and a human will.

These two wills, distinct according to their natures but united according to the person, must be firmly held for the salvation of our souls. Whoever dares to dissent from this faith shall be excluded from the communion of the Church.

Furthermore, all the bishops and clergy of the provinces of Africa and Numidia who took part in this synod sign and testify.

Bishop Gregory of Carthage
Bishop Fulgentius of Ruspe
Bishop Maximus of Thysdrus
Bishop Victorius of Mactaris
Bishop Fortunatus of Tubursica
Bishop Faustinus of Vultur
Bishop Urbanus of Hippo Regius
Bishop Martin of Achrida
Bishop Victor of Zana
Bishop Paulus of Alba

1

LETTER I

Letter to the Emperor Constans II from the African bishops
646 AD

To our most glorious lord Constans Augustus, by the grace of God, and to us reverend brothers and holy bishops of Africa and Numidia, greetings.

We have heard, most august Caesar, that many heretics, the Monothelites, have arisen who claim that there is only one will in Christ our Lord Jesus Christ. We believe it is our duty, according to the Word of God and the orthodox tradition of the Church, to inform you, defender of the faith, of our belief. In one Christ there are two wills, divine and human, which are distinct according to their natures but united according to the person; and we must firmly hold this, so that our souls may be saved by this faith. Those who hold contrary beliefs are anathema from the Church of God. We humbly commend this our faith, which is established in the Catholic faith, to you, so that you and your entire realm may diligently preserve it.

Furthermore, all the bishops, priests, and clerics who attended this synod sign by name, testifying to this holy faith in Christ our Lord Jesus.

2

LETTER II

**First Letter to Pope Vitalian from the African bishops.
Gregory, Archbishop of Carthage**
Unknown date 646 AD

Venerable father, most blessed Pope Vitalian, greetings in the Lord.

We, the bishops, priests, and clergy of the province of Africa, gathered unanimously in synod, give thanks to your holiness and the labor you undertake for the Catholic faith in Christ our Lord Jesus Christ. In this synod, we firmly declare and confess that there are two wills in one Christ our Lord Jesus Christ: namely, a divine will and a human will, which are distinct according to their natures but united according to the person. We will not depart from this faith, which has been handed down by the apostles and has come to us through the holy Catholic Church. Whoever denies this faith shall be anathema from the Church of God. We humbly ask, most holy father, that this our belief be confirmed by your authority and promoted throughout the universal Church.

Furthermore, all the bishops, priests, and clergy who attended this synod sign by name, testifying to the truth of this faith.

3

LETTER III

**Second Letter to Pope Vitalian from the African bishops.
Gregory, Archbishop of Carthage**
Unknown date

To the holy and most blessed Father, our Lord Pope Vitalian, bishops and priests of the province of Africa, greetings and prayer in the Lord.

Venerable Father, most holy pontiff, we, the bishops and priests of the province of Africa, gathered in unanimous consent in the Catholic faith, greet your holiness and give thanks for your diligence in safeguarding the truth in our Lord Jesus Christ. We humbly commend this sincere profession of our faith to you, so that both you and your entire church may know that we stand firm in the apostolic doctrine and the traditions of the holy Catholic Church. We affirm that in Christ there are two wills, divine and human, distinct according to natures and united according to person. Against the Monothelite heretics, who say that there is only one will in Christ, we firmly and unanimously declare the orthodox Catholic faith.

We ask that this confession of our faith be confirmed by your holiness and promoted throughout the entire church, so that the salvation of our souls may be preserved.

Farewell in the Lord, most holy Father.

Subscription of the bishops:
Gregory, bishop of Carthage;
Maximus, bishop of Thysdrus;
Victorius, bishop of Macta;
Fortunatus, bishop of Tubursis;
Urbanus, bishop of Hippo;
Martinus, bishop of Achrida;
Victor, bishop of Zana;
Paulus, bishop of Alba.

4

LETTER IV

Letter to Pope Agatho from the African bishops Gregory, Archbishop of Carthage
Unknown date

To the holy and most blessed Father, our Lord Pope Agatho, bishops and priests of the province of Africa, greetings and prayers in the Lord.

Venerable Father, most holy Pontiff, we, the bishops and priests of the province of Africa, gathered unanimously in the Catholic faith, greet your holiness and desire your grace. We confess to you, most holy Father, that your wisdom and diligence preserve the entire body of the Catholic Church in faith and unity. In Christ alone, we confess that there are two wills, divine and human, according to distinct natures, and according to the person, unity. Against the Monothelite heretics, who assert that there is only one will in Christ, we firmly and unanimously defend the Catholic faith. We ask you, most holy Father, to deign to strengthen our confession of faith with your confirmation, so that the whole Church may know that we stand in orthodoxy.

Farewell in the Lord, most holy Father.

Subscription of the bishops:
Gregory, Bishop of Carthage;
Maximus, Bishop of Thysdrus;
Victorius, Bishop of Mactar;
Fortunatus, Bishop of Tubursis;
Urbanus, Bishop of Hippo;
Martinus, Bishop of Achrida;
Victor, Bishop of Zana;
Paul, Bishop of Alba.

5

LETTER V

**First Papal Letter responding to the African Church
Pope Agatho, Bishop of Rome**
May, 18, 678 AD

Agatho, bishop, servant of the servants of God, to all bishops, priests, and deacons, to the entire clergy and Catholic people established throughout Africa, greetings in the Lord.

Our spirit rejoices in the Lord, hearing your firm confession of faith, by which you not only detest the impiety of the Monothelites but also show that you steadfastly hold to the standard of Catholic truth established by the holy fathers. Therefore, we, rejoicing in every way, give thanks to God, who has worked in you such a guardianship of faith that in such a long interval of time you have neither departed from the truth nor forsaken the communion of the apostolic see, your mother. We therefore congratulate you, dearest brothers, and exhort you in the Lord to persevere in what you have begun, keeping the apostolic faith intact, and presenting yourselves as a living sacrifice to God, blameless for the holy Catholic Church.

Given at Rome, on the 13th day before the Kalends of June, under the reign of our lord Constantine Augustus, in the 10th year, in the 3rd indiction.

6

LETTER VI

Second Papal Letter responding to the African Church
Pope Agatho, Bishop of Rome
June 21, 668 AD

Agatho, bishop, servant of the servants of God, to his beloved brothers and co-bishops Gregory, Maximus, Victorius, Fortunatus, Urbanus, Martin, Victor, Paul, and to all the sons of the holy Catholic and Apostolic Church established throughout Africa, greetings in the Lord.

Your letter of holiness has brought us great joy, dearest brothers, which you have sent full of Catholic faith by unanimous consent. For in it we read that apostolic rule, which our blessed fathers preserved, and you, inspired by divine grace, have held unchanged in every part.

The holy and apostolic Roman Church has given you great praise for not having departed from the unity of the mother church in such great tribulations of the times and in the adversity of the barbarians, nor have you become estranged from its doctrine.

Therefore, we give thanks to the Lord, who has established you in the pillar of truth, and has set your confession as an example for all the churches of the East and West.

Stand firm and hold to the traditions which you received through the apostles and the holy fathers, in which we also desire to stand, together with you, for the glory of the name of Jesus Christ.

Given on the ninth day before the Kalends of July, under the rule of Lord Constantine, in the tenth year, in the third indiction, in Rome.

7

LETTER VII

Third Papal Letter responding to the African Church
Pope Agatho, Bishop of Rome
July 11, 668 AD

 Agatho, bishop, servant of the servants of God, to Gregory, bishop of Carthage, Maximus of Thysdrus, Victorius of Mactis, Fortunatus of Tubursis, Urbanus of Hippo, Martin of Achrida, Victorius of Zana, Paul of Alba, and to all bishops and the entire clergy and Catholic people established throughout Africa, greetings and apostolic blessing. We praise and glorify our Lord Jesus Christ, who has strengthened you in His faith and brought you to the full confession of truth by His grace. We have received your letter, full of apostolic faith, with great joy, in which we recognized the profession of Catholic truth and understood that you abominate the heresy of the Monothelites. For in such great tribulation, in which your church is now surrounded, we have greatly admired your perseverance in the doctrine of the holy fathers.

May the peace of our Lord Jesus Christ be with you, dearest brothers, and with all your flock, and our prayer for your steadfastness is continually poured out to God. We urge you to hold firmly to the traditions of the Church, which the apostolic see has always preserved and strived to maintain, so that you may remain with one voice and one mind in the confession of Christ.

Given in Rome, on the fourth day before the Ides of July, in the tenth year of the reign of our lord Constantine, in the third indiction.

8

LETTER VIII

**Letter of the Bishops of Africa to the Apostolic See
Honorius, Bishop of Capsa**
March 699 AD

To the most blessed and most holy father in Christ, our lord pope, we, a few surviving bishops established in Africa, send eternal greetings in the Lord.

Although, alas, due to the invasion of the Agarene people and the constant persecutions that afflict our region, and have devastated the churches of Christ, so that most are desolate and their pastors are either exiled or deceased, we nevertheless give thanks to our Lord God, who has not allowed us to perish with the wicked, nor to depart from the Catholic faith. We keep intact the faith of the holy and apostolic Roman Church, which has been handed down by the apostles, and we wholeheartedly embrace and hold the orthodox confession that was made in the holy council of Constantinople against the Monothelites. Neither has any heresy corrupted us, nor has the communion of heretics stained us, but we strive to persist in the tradition of the holy fathers, and we firmly embrace the judgment of your apostolic see, as the head and foundation of the Church.

We humbly beseech you, most blessed father, that although we have been almost brought to nothing due to our sins and the very serious tribulation of our times, you may deem us worthy to remain in communion with your holiness, and that the apostolic see may remember its sons, even if they are remote and few, and situated in distress. We also pray that, if possible, you may deem it fitting to send words of consolation through your holy letters, so that we may receive strength in the Lord, and that the remnants of the Lord's flock may not fail amid temporal tribulations.

This letter was given, by God's command, in the place called Capsa, in the fourteenth year of the reign of King Cordan [the Caliphate]i, in the month of March, in the eleventh indiction.

Subscribed:
Honorius, bishop of Capsa
Faustinus, bishop of Cebarsensis
Paulus, bishop of Vegensis
Felix, bishop of Macomensis
Restitutus, bishop of Cirtense
and many others, whose names have been erased due to the calamity of the times.

9

LETTER IX

Fragmentary Letter of the African bishops
Unknown
June 23, 700?

To our most blessed father, guardian of the holy apostolic see, eternal salvation in the Lord.

[...] Affected by very serious persecutions, we nonetheless remain steadfast in the Catholic faith, nor have we deviated from the traditions of the holy fathers. [...] Our Church, although surrounded by infidel nations, maintains unity with the apostolic see and holds the orthodox confession of Christ, the Son of God, publicly professed. [...] you, dearest father, are remembered in our prayers, and we always await your help.

Given on the ninth day before the kalends of July, in the year of the reign of King Cordani, in the eleventh indiction.

Uncertain subscription:
[...] bishops, clergy, and all the faithful of the province of Africa.

10

LETTER X

Papal Letter to the African Clergy
Pope Gregory II, Bishop of Rome
August 715 AD

Gregory, bishop, servant of the servants of God, to the beloved brothers, bishops and clergy of the province of Africa, greetings and apostolic blessing.

Beloved brothers in Christ, we have heard of your sadness and the persecutions you endure in your land, from the nations that do not know the name of Christ. Do not lose heart, but take strength in the Lord. Do not abandon the holy church of God, which you also protect, nor deviate from the truth of the apostolic faith, nor stray from the traditions of the holy fathers. As far as we are able, we always pray for you and strive to provide assistance for your stability. Remain in perpetual communion and charity in the Lord.

Given at Rome, in the basilica of Saint Peter, in the year of the Lord's incarnation 715, in the month of August, in the third indiction.

11

LETTER XI

Papal Letter to the African Clergy
Pope Gregory III, Bishop of Rome
October 735 AD

Gregory, bishop, servant of the servants of God, to the beloved brothers, bishops and clergy of the province of Africa, greeting and apostolic blessing.

Dearest brothers in Christ, we have heard of the tribulations and persecutions that you are suffering in your land from the nations that do not know the name of Christ. Do not falter in faith, but remain steadfast and always stable in the Lord. Preserve the holy Church of

God, which you guard, with an orthodox confession of apostolic faith, and do not deviate from it. We offer our prayers for you daily, that the Lord may strengthen and protect you. May you remain in perpetual communion and charity in the Lord.

Given at Rome, in the basilica of Saint Peter, in the year of the Lord's incarnation 735, in the month of October, in the sixth indiction.

12

LETTER XII

To the most excellent lord King Charles from the holy bishop from Africa.
Unknown, Archbishop of Carthage
Unknown date, 780? AD

Most excellent lord, most glorious and most pious son in Christ, King Charles, we give thanks to God that the most gracious God has granted us such a king through our prayers, by whom the Catholic faith is exalted, and the holy church, which the enemy and unclean spirit do not cease to disturb through treacherous and sacrilegious men, strives to be restored.

Therefore, we give thanks to your piety that you reign in such a way that you not only govern the kingdom with earthly authority, but also, which is far greater, you extend the Catholic faith. And although we are physically separated, yet with one spirit, one faith, one love, and one worship, we confess, adore, and venerate our Lord Jesus Christ.

Hence, we ask your piety to take such concern for us as you deem worthy for your own salvation, so that the holy Roman church, our mother, to which we turn for certain care due to ancient custom, may be consoled in the integrity of faith and the fullness of Catholic truth through your prayers and assistance.

For many are the tribulations of the righteous, and the Lord will deliver them from all these. For we, though oppressed, have not been overcome; though afflicted, we have not despaired. Be mindful, most pious king, of the churches of God that are in Africa; be mindful of the bishops, priests, deacons, and all the members of the church who are pressed by pressure and affliction.

For you are, after God, our hope and consolation. Therefore, we beseech your clemency to deign to lend an ear of your piety to our prayers, and to devote prayers for us to the Lord Jesus Christ, who made you reign, that He may deign to deliver us from these tribulations.

May the Lord preserve your life and your kingdom in all good works, and after the course of this life, grant you eternal life with all the saints. Amen.

13

LETTER XIII

LETTER TO THOMAS, ARCHBISHOP OF CARTHAGE

Epistle of St. Leo IX to Thomas the African bishop. He pointed out that the Carthaginian archbishop was the leader of all Africa. The bishop of Gummitan was ordered to consecrate the bishops by consent, nor to sit in the provincial council; to depose the Roman pontificate and to depose the bishops and to appoint general councils.

IN THE YEAR 1053

Bishop Leo, servant of God's servants, to Thomas, his beloved brother and co-bishop.

When we recall, on the authority of the venerable canons, that two hundred and five bishops were present at the Carthaginian council, and when we hear from your fraternity that scarcely five bishops survived in all of Africa, certainly in the third part of this corruptible world, we sympathize with all the entrails of our soul at your great loss. But when we learn that the very remains of Christianity were taught to be dispersed by mutual dissension, and to be inflamed against each other by zeal and contention, another thing first occurred to us to say, like that of the most holy Amos: Spare me, Lord, spare me, I beseech you: who will raise up Jacob, because he is a parent? (Am. 7) But although we are very sorry for such and such a lack of religion; We rejoice greatly, however, because you demand the sixty-seventh of your mother, the holy Roman Church, and expound upon your questions; religious beginning You know, therefore, without a doubt that, after the Roman pontiff, the first archbishop and greatest metropolitan of all Africa is the bishop of Carthage, and that, whoever he may be, that Bishop of Gummuitan has no license to consecrate bishops, or to depose, or to convene a provincial council of Babel, without the consent of the archbishop of Carthage, whose dignity or power let it be, with the exception of those which belong to the proper parish; Forever, he will act with the advice of the Carthaginian archbishop, just as he did with the African bishop there. Our fellow-bishops Peter and John of Undecharissin feel correctly about the dignity of the Carthaginian Church, and they do not agree with the error of the Gummitan Church. I do not want this to be hidden from you before, that it should not be left aside from the decision of the Roman Pontiff that a universal council should be held, or that bishops should be condemned and deposed; but you are permitted to examine certain bishops, and you are not permitted to give a definitive opinion without consulting the Roman Pontiff, as has been said: which, if you seek, you can find in the holy canons. For although it was said by the Lord to all the apostles in general: Whatever shall be bound on earth shall be bound in heaven (Matt. 18), yet it was not without reason that Blessed Peter, the chief of the apostles, was said to Peter the chief of the apostles: You are Peter, and on this rock I will build my church :

and I will owe you the keys of the ruler of the heavens (Matt. 16). And in another place: Strengthen your brothers (Luke 22). Of course, because the greatest and most difficult cases of all the churches are to be defined by the saint and principal B. Peter, his successors. Now that we have decided to answer the questions also of our brother bishops Peter and John; we pray that your holy fraternity will not constantly watch over the mutilations of the holy Catholic Church, and devoutly pray for us, always preserve the holy and individual Trinity, most dear brother.

Given on the 16th day of January, in the fifth year of Leo IX, of the seventh indictment.

14

LETTER XIV

LETTER TO PETER & JOHN, PRIESTS OF THE AFRICAN CHURCH

St. Leo IX praises the bishops Peter and John for having held a council on ecclesiastical matters at their command and for defending the rights of the archbishop of Carthage against the bishop of Gummitan.

IN THE YEAR 1053

Bishop Leo, servant of the servants of God, greetings and apostolic blessing to the beloved brothers in Christ, the bishops Peter and John.

We lament the fact that the African Churches are so congregated with agents that only barely five bishops can be found, where once two hundred and five were used to be counted by plenary councils;

and there the Lord's innumerable flock of many sheep, under numerous rams, rejoiced in high peace. But imputing these things to our sins, lets us fear the justice of the Creator, and earnestly ask for his mercy, that he may at last deign to look upon our servants. But what you wrote to us, thanking the Lord for the state of the holy Roman Church and our safety, you begged: you will know that we thank your fraternity, and always pray for your consolation. And truly, brethren, this is acceptable to our Lord Jesus Christ, that he should look upon and visit the head of all wonders; but the members seek and desire without ceasing the safety of their head. You have indeed done well in that you have held a council on ecclesiastical affairs, which we ordered you to do every year or once. Moreover, you rightly defended the dignity of the Carthaginian church against the Gummitan bishop; because without a doubt the first archbishop after the Roman pontiff and the whole of Africa can lose the privilege once suspected by the holy Roman and apostolic see: but he will maintain it until the end of the age, and until the name of our Lord Jesus Christ is invoked in it, whether Carthage lies desolate or rises glorious sometimes. This is clearly shown from the council of the blessed martyr Cyprian, this from the synod of Aurelius, this from all the African councils, this, which is greater, from the painstaking decrees of our venerable predecessors, the Romans, is clearly shown. Archbishop of Carthage, of whatever rank or power he may be. The Gummitan bishop will only take care of what belongs to his own parish; and the rest, like the other African bishops, will act by the advice of the Archbishop of Carthage, who alone in Africa usually has the mantle from the apostolic see. Under and bishops retain the principal and ancient right of consecration, as it cannot be understood from the words of Aurelius in the Council of Carthage (Council. Carth. III) chapter thirty, when he says: In the church, to which your sanctities have been deigned to assemble, I believe and almost throughout the diam Dominica we have to order bishops, etc. But do not let this be hidden from you, do not deny the opinion of the Roman pontiff to be held apart from knowledge, or to be condemned or deposed by the bishops; it is not allowed to give Which, if you seek, you can find established in the holy councils: namely, because the greater and more difficult causes of all the Churches, through the holy and principal of the blessed Peter, are to be diffused from his successors, since it is to whom it is divinely given: Strengthen your brothers (Luke 22); and: I will give you the keys of the kingdom of heaven (Matt. 16), etc.

Now, since you require our opinion about the archbishops and metropolitans, the statements of our venerable fathers clearly show it, that is: Clement, Anacletus, Anicetus, and others, where it is also read: they were collated, and they did not teach the apostles. But the order of bishops is one, although some are pitied by others, either because they retain the first states and more named, according to the power or laws of the age, or because they can obtain some privilege of dignity from the holy Fathers for some events of sanctity. For, just as every worldly power is distant from one another in these degrees of dignity, that is to say, Augustus or the emperor is the first, then the Caesars, then kings, leaders and counts and judges; so also, the ecclesiastical dignity ordained by the holy Fathers is found, saying blessed Clement (*Epistle. 1, tom. 1., p. 91*): In these states, in which once great men were their priests and the first teachers of the law, primates or patriarchs were placed, who would justly avoid the rest of the judgments and the greater affairs, who also died not of one province, but of many. Where the heathen archbishops go, Christian archbishops are appointed to preside over each province. But where there was a metropolis, which is interpreted as a mother city, there were metropolitans: they would preside over some province of the greater and matriarchal states from three or four states. These are sometimes only remembered as metropolitans, and sometimes as archbishops, if there were no greater ones in the province. But where the smaller states had only priests or counts, they were appointed bishops. Moreover, the tribunes of the people do not mean deaf priests, or priests of the lower order of the clergy. The Roman Pontiff was preferred to all these by divine and human privilege. The primates of Africa must be understood differently, because anciently primates were established in each of its provinces, not according to the power of any state, but according to the time of their ordination. but one presides over all of them, that is, the Archbishop of Carthage, who also may not incongruously be called a metropolitan, to prophesy Carthage as the metropolis of all Africa, of which we have mentioned above. Thus, it is read in the Council of Carthage: "The bishop of the first see shall not be called chief priest, or high priest, or anything of the sort, but only the bishop of the first see." Constantly watching over your holy brotherhood with the armies of God's holy Church and praying devoutly for us, may the holy and individual Trinity always preserve it, dearest brothers.

15

LETTER XIV

To the Christian People of Africa and to Cyriacus, the Archbishop of Carthage
Pope Gregory VII, Bishop of Rome
Sept. 16, 1073

The Apostle has declared it, exclaims the Pope, every man is subject to superior powers. Now as we must obey earthly powers, how much more should we not obey the spiritual power which replaces here below Jesus Christ himself. I write these things to you my dearest sons, pain in the heart and tears in the eyes. It has reached our ears that a part of you are revolting against the law of Christ and against our venerable brother Cyriacus, your archbishop, your master. Christ has accused him before the Saracens outraged him with his insults to the point that treated like a thief; he was stripped naked and beaten. O fatal example! Shame on you and on the entire Church of Christ, that is once again captive again. He is condemned on false testimony struck like the thieves, and those who claim to still believe in his incarnation venerate his passion and respect his mysteries. I cannot remain silent. I will raise my voice against you. I do not want your sins to be thrown at the feet of my terrible Judge. But as you do not know, you cannot come to me easily because of the length and dangers of sea voyages and that I cannot discern from here the part of malice and ignorance. I open to you the bowels of mercy. May your regrets bring a balm to my sadness. Return to better feelings, otherwise I will strike you without pity in the name of Saint Peter and of mine from the sword of excommunication.

I have learned through your letters, venerable brother, of the pain caused to you by the pagans and the lost children of the Church. I have cordially sympathized with them. You, therefore, have to endure a double battle: you must watch out for the secret pitfalls of the Christians, and endure the persecution of the Saracens, which threaten not only this perishable body but the faith itself. What in fact is it to ask a priest to break divine law at the order of a power of this world, if not to ask him to deny his faith. But thanks be to God, the firmness of your conviction appeared to all like a luminous beacon in the midst of the darkness of this degraded nation. You suffered in your membership, but your confession would have been even more precious if under the very blows which struck you, confounding the error and publishing the doctrine of Christ, you had shed to the last drop of your blood. This is it, venerable brother, we do not hide it from you what we owe to faith and truth our entire body and our life. We end with affection in these terms. We cannot be present personally with you, venerable brother, but our thoughts do not leave you. We will write to you on all suitable occasions. We will urgently pray to the

God of mercies so that he designs to help this unfortunate Church of Africa, which has been battered for so long by the waves and the storm.

16

LETTER XV

**Letter to Anzir, King of Mauritania
Pope Gregory VII, Bishop of Rome**
1076/1077

Gregory, bishop, servant of the servants of God, to Anzir, king of Mauretania of the Sitifienne province of Africa. Greetings and apostolic blessing.

Your Nobility wrote to us this year to ask us to consecrate bishop according to the Christian constitutions the priest Servaus which we hastened to do because your request was just You at the same time sent us gifts you out of deference to the blessed Peter prince of the apostles and out of love for us redeemed the Christians who were captive among you and promised to redeem those who would still be found

God the creator of all things without whom we can do absolutely nothing has obviously inspired you with this goodness and disposed your heart to this generous act. The Almighty God who wants all men to be saved and that none perish does not in fact approve of anything more among us that the love of our fellow men after the love that we owe to him and that the observation of this precept Do to others what you would have done to you We must more particularly than other peoples practice this virtue of charity you and us who in different forms adore the same unique God and who every day we praise and venerate in him the creator of the centuries and the master of the world. The nobles of the city of Rome having learned from us the act that God inspired in you admire the elevation of your heart and publish your praises Two of them, our most usual companions Alberic and Cencius, raised with us from their adolescence in the palace of Rome, would very much like to become friends and reciprocal services with you They would be happy to be able to please you in this country They are sending you some of their men who will tell you how much their masters have esteem for your experience and your greatness and how much they will be satisfied to serve you here We recommend them to Your Magnificence and we ask for them this love and this devotion that we will always have for you and for everything that concerns you God knows that the honor of the Almighty God inspires the friendship that we have dedicated to you and how well we wish your salvation and your glory in this life and in the next. We pray from the bottom of our hearts to receive you after a long life in the bosom of the blessedness of the most holy patriarch Abraham.

17

LETTER XVI

Letter to the Archbishop of Pisa
Abd- Allah Ibn Abu Khoracan
1157

Abd Allah Ibn Abu Khoraçan to the illustrious and very noble archbishop of Pisa Villain primate of Corsica and Sardinia to the illustrious sheiks, former consuls, notable counts and to all the people of the city may God guide them In the name of a clement and merciful God We offer you our most affectionate and distinguished greetings. We honor your nation, of which flattering things are said to us every day as a result of the bonds of friendship and goodwill that have existed for a long time between our countries and which have led to fraternal relations. between our two peoples We have received the gracious letters that you sent us by the illustrious sheik the reïs Abou Temim Meimoun son of Guillaume your ambassador man of such great prudence skill etc. We praise your high wisdom for having sent us such a man who took care with intelligence and tireless dedication of what was contained in your letter and of everything that concerns the honor and interests of your commune As it is the sign of friendship to inform one's friends of the state of one's affairs we let you know who are those we love most in the Christian world that

God delivered us and our State from the invasion of the Masmouda of the Almohads 2 We repelled their armies and we killed many of our enemies You tell us about a galley that came from Alexandria to Tunis which was well received by us although it would have harmed the Pisans here is the truth about this incident We had sent a racing galley to sea when heavy weather pushed it into the port of Alexandria She was well received and well treated there. We could not respond with ingratitude to this good process. Also, an Egyptian galley, having come to Tunis shortly after, received good treatment there, she got supplies there and sold some of her prisoners there. and brought the others back to his departure. We did not know that this galley had captured several Pisans. If we had been informed of this we would have eagerly redeemed the prisoners with our own funds to hand them over to your honorable sheiks as a testimony of our friendship. For the rest we have remedied for the future to similar inconveniences and made such a thing impossible for all those who deal with the sale of captives and slaves in our countries This means that the emir forbade the sale of captives and prisoners of Pisan nationality in his kingdom 22 As for this duty that it is customary to levy here on the grains, namely five hand knuckles per bag, it must be reduced We have decided that in the future we will have to be content with taking four handles on the top of each bag We have also agreed on the subject of goods that your merchants could not sell in our country and on which we nevertheless collected as on the goods sold one for ten that no duties would be required in the future and that they could be obtained freely Regarding the alum imported by the Pisans no duties will be required in the future We have ordered that all your merchants their factors their families their employees or servants who live between the wall of the city of Tunis and the enclosure of their fondouk or their houses are treated with respect and with affectionate attention We have given the assurance to the sheik the reïs Abou Temim and this will be done thus We have also ordered that any Pisan prisoner or slave found in our lands be delivered or ransomed in my name and sent to Pisa at liberty Your envoy has promised us reciprocity We have thus removed all subjects of dispute between us We have stopped all these things with your honorable envoy the illustrious sheik the reïs Abou Temim by a firm and irrevocable act that we have sincerely and in good form ratified We have entrusted to the same envoy the letter that we address to Your Lordships may God increase their glory with the verbal response to the requests of the republic that his eloquence will expose to them when he sees them again We end by sending you our most cordial greetings for the great and for the small, for the nobles and for the people God is our hope and our best protector.

18

LETTER XVII

Letter to the Archbishop of Pisa
Abd- Allah Ibn Abu Khoracan
1157

Abd Allah Ibn Abu Khoraçan to the illustrious and very noble archbishop of Pisa Villain primate of Corsica and Sardinia to the illustrious sheiks, former consuls, notable counts and to all the people of the city may God guide them In the name of a clement and merciful God. We offer you our most affectionate and distinguished greetings. We honor your nation, of which flattering things are said to us every day as a result of the bonds of friendship and goodwill that have existed for a long time between our countries and which have led to fraternal relations. between our two peoples. We have received the gracious letters that you sent us by the illustrious sheik the reïs Abou Temim Meimoun son of Guillaume your ambassador man of such great prudence skill etc. We praise your high wisdom for having sent us such a man who took care with intelligence and tireless dedication of what was contained in your letter and of everything that concerns the honor and interests of your commune. As it is the sign of friendship to inform one's friends of the state of one's affairs we let you know who are those we love most in the Christian world that

God delivered us and our State from the invasion of the Masmouda of the Almohads. We repelled their armies and we killed many of our enemies. You tell us about a galley that came from Alexandria to Tunis which was well received by us although it would have harmed the Pisans here is the truth about this incident We had sent a racing galley to sea when heavy weather pushed it into the port of Alexandria She was well received and well treated there. We could not respond with ingratitude to this good process. Also, an Egyptian galley, having come to Tunis shortly after, received good treatment there, she got supplies there and sold some of her prisoners there. and brought the others back to his departure. We did not know that this galley had captured several Pisans. If we had been informed of this we would have eagerly redeemed the prisoners with our own funds to hand them over to your honorable sheiks as a testimony of our friendship. For the rest we have remedied for the future to similar inconveniences and made such a thing impossible for all those who deal with the sale of captives and slaves in our countries. This means that the emir forbade the sale of captives and prisoners of Pisan nationality in his kingdom. As for this duty that it is customary to levy here on the grains, namely five hand knuckles per bag, it must be reduced. We have decided that in the future we will have to be content with taking four handles on the top of each bag. We have also agreed on the subject of goods that your merchants could not sell in our country and on which we nevertheless collected as on the goods sold one for ten that no duties would be required in the future and that they could be obtained freely. Regarding the alum imported by the Pisans no duties will be required in the future. We have ordered that all your merchants their factors their families their employees or servants who live between the wall of the city of Tunis and the enclosure of their fondouk or their houses are treated with respect and with affectionate attention. We have given the assurance to the sheik the reïs Abou Temim and this will be done thus. We have also ordered that any Pisan prisoner or slave found in our lands be delivered or ransomed in my name and sent to Pisa at liberty. Your envoy has promised us reciprocity. We have thus removed all subjects of dispute between us. We have stopped all these things with your honorable envoy the illustrious sheik the reïs Abou Temim by a firm and irrevocable act that we have sincerely and in good form ratified. We have entrusted to the same envoy the letter that we address to Your Lordships may God increase their glory with the verbal response to the requests of the republic that his eloquence will expose to them when he sees them again. We end by sending you our most cordial greetings for the great and for the small, for the nobles and for the people God is our hope and our best protector.

19

LETTER XVIII

Letter to the Republic of Pisa and it's Consul Abd el-Ouahid

Sept. 9, 1211

To the illustrious consul Geoffroy Visconti prince of Pisa on behalf of Abd el Ouahid son of sheik Abou Hafs. May God grant a perpetual and glorious victory to our lord the imam the caliph In Nacer-li-din-illah the prince of believers, offspring of the caliphs, etc, etc. We received your letter and we saw in it the promise to scrupulously and faithfully observe the patti conditions agreed with the powerful Government. Your Ambassador Gérard told us everything that you had particularly recommended to him regarding your constant and commendable care to maintain a good peace between us and the recommendations that you make to all those who leave your countries to respect the Muslims and their property to avoid causing them any harm or deceiving them. The effect of your intentions was already evident by the conduct of the travelers your compatriots and that of all your people. Also the treaty stipulated with you is extremely well regarded by the Almohads and your eagerness to maintain it known to everyone. Here we act the same with all those who come from you or who enjoy your protection.

20

LETTER XIX

To the King of Morocco
Pope Innocent III
March 8, 1198

Innocent, bishop, servant of the servants of God, to the illustrious Emir al-moumenin, king of Morocco and to his subjects. May they come to know the truth and may they persevere in it for their greatest advantage. Among the merciful works recommended by Our Lord Jesus Christ in the Gospel to his faithful the redemption of the captives is not the last. We must therefore grant apostolic protection to those who dedicate themselves to such works Generous men among whom are the bearers of our presents letters have recently given themselves, under divine inspiration, the law and the obligation to devote a third of what they possess and will possess in the future to the redemption of captives. In order to more completely realize their project, they were allowed to also redeem pagan captives. so that they can sometimes by means of exchanges remove from slavery some Christian captives. As such a work can only be advantageous to pagans and Christians, we thought it appropriate to inform you of it through these apostolic letters May He who is the seeing the truth and life makes you recognize the truth, that is to say Christ, and leads you to it as soon as possible. Given in Lateran on the 8th of the Ides of March, second year of our pontificate.

21

LETTER XX

To the Arab Peoples residing on the Island of Sicily
Pope Innocent III, Bishop of Rome
1199/1200

Innocent, bishop, servant of the servants of God, to the Saracens living in Sicily, may they be devoted to us and may they continue to be faithful to the King. We have learned with joy that you have always maintained towards your masters the loyalty that you owe them. We desire especially that you retain today these feelings towards our dear son in Christ Frederick King of Sicily and that you resist the solicitations and the violence of Marcuald You know by experience the cruelty of the tyrant only those are spared that he cannot reach You know how he caused priests to be thrown into the sea how he condemned others to prison or to the stake Judge what such a man would do against Saracens. He would crack down with all the more fury against them as he would believe he had to shed pagan blood to make himself acceptable to God. By ignoring the father who removed him from dust and dung he showed what he is capable of. If you did not reject his advances your property and your riches would become prey to his people. Would he who has violated public oaths with us observe the promises he makes to you because he needs your assistance? See the truth and keep the faithfulness of your fathers, do not be ungrateful, do not forget the benefits of the kings of Sicily with regard to your nation and know that the Holy Apostolic See wants, not only to preserve, but to increase the freedoms and rights that you enjoy, if you keep the faith and devotion that you owe to him.

For these purposes, we send to Sicily the cardinal of Saint Laurent in Lucina, the archbishop of Naples, and the archbishop of Taranto. We send at the same time our dear cousins marshal Jacques and Otho of Palombaria with a strong army which will easily overcome Marcuald.

22

LETTER XXI

To the King of Morocco regarding the Christians of Africa
Pope Innocent IV, Bishop of Rome
Oct. 21, 1246

To the illustrious king of Morocco.

We greatly congratulate your majesty, says the Pope, that following the example of the Christian princes and in accordance with your own acts and the acts of your predecessors who have conferred possessions and numerous privileges on the Church of Morocco. For you have not only defended this Church against the attacks of malicious people opposed to the Christian faith, but also increased its immunities, and its privileges, and granted to the Christians called by your predecessors new favors and considerable benefits. We also hope that you are willing to protect even more of the pious establishments and the Christians who are in your states. The world will thus know that your name is no less glorious than that of your fathers and we, concerned about your interests, will use all the efforts of ecclesiastical power to preserve you from the attack of your enemies. You have fierce and powerful enemies who seek to seize your kingdom through machinations and through weapons. Christians, knowing well that heavenly assistance rather than numbers gives victory, have until now energetically resisted them and have often triumphed over them for the defense of their faith and your states. They do not spare themselves, and you know that more than once they have left a large number of their own on the battlefields. But it is possible that one day ruse and a sudden invasion will surprise, and find them poorly prepared. We can fear that in the long run, numbers do not outweigh value. We must prevent by an effective measure such a misfortune as disastrous for Christians as for your kingdom. We therefore pray to Your Serenity to give Christians some fortified places where they can take refuge in difficult times. Ask you to entrust them with the guarding of a few seaports, through which they can, if necessary, move away and return with new resources to your aid.

This work was produced in association with:

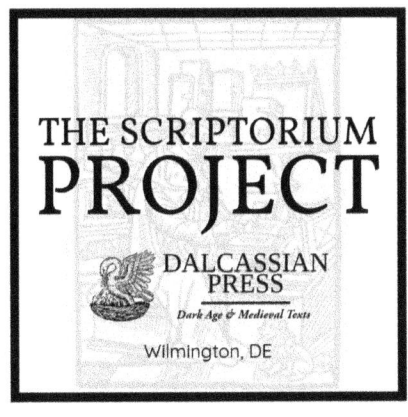

www.ingramcontent.com/pod-product-compliance
Lightning Source LLC
LaVergne TN
LVHW061049070526
838201LV00074B/5229